I AM

DECLARATION and MEDITATION
Devotional

Apostle Ivy N. Springer

For accompaniment audio of
I Am Declarations visit,
www.ivynspringer.com

The Barber Shoppe Marketing Salon, LLC.
Atlanta, Georgia
www.thebarbershoppeatl.com

DEDICATION

He is second to none, my very patient husband, Thomas E.
Springer. Thank you so very much for being my biggest fan
and supporter in everything I do. Your faith is contagious
and I Am better because of you.

To my sister, Joy Blackamore, of Joyful Empowerment,
thank you for being my sounding board and my
JOYful motivation.

To my children, Candice and Thomas, my grandchildren,
nieces, nephews and spiritual sons and daughters,
my prayer is that the application of the principles written
within will transform our lineage in such a way that not only
will your names be great, but you will be philanthropist who
trail-blaze a legacy of kingdom building that will bless and
bring you joy, as well as others for generations to come.
To Spirit of Love Life Empowerment International, your
confidence in my leadership truly inspires me.

Apostle Ivy N. Springer

CONTENTS

FOREWORD

Our relationship with the Apostle Ivy N. Springer began nearly 30 years ago, when we received a beautiful gift of a bible from her mother, Clarissa Blackamore. That bible sits on the nightstand in our bedroom and has great sentimental value. Our relationship with the Blackamore-Springer family marked the beginning of a spiritual re-birth in the both of us. Raised in religious households, we felt we knew God, but this was something different. This relationship began us on a journey of intimacy with God. Indeed, the guidance and unwavering love of Clarissa, Ivy, Joy and John had a profound impact on us and affected us in ways that were new and wonderful. Clarissa married us 26 years ago at Northwestern University's Garrett Seminary Chapel. Our relationship continued as did our collective journey in Christ. Being honored to write a foreword for this volume is humbling indeed. What can we say? How can we contribute? However, those doubts are our own: not borne of God or His Word. Therefore, we will share with you some brief and personal thoughts that will hopefully embed these words as a map with which to navigate through your life. They have indeed helped us.

Over the last few decades we have witnessed man's inhumanity to man. We have stopped valuing each other and stopped considering how to love and cherish our differences. Not a day goes by when we don't think of our blessings. We are proud parents. We have both gone on to earn doctor of philosophy degrees in our fields and contribute both professionally and personally to our respective academic communities. Indeed, we have been blessed in ways that are amazing and empowering. In the academy, we are taught to think critically, question and examine. One constant for us is that despite the training, one thing we don't question or criticize is the wonder of God. For us, His teachings are a way of life. As such, this book is a tool. It provides a way to make the impossible possible, a way to imagine the unimaginable and a way to remember to bless others through your often forgotten or neglected gifts.

No doubt we are faced with daily challenges. Challenges that sometimes make us wonder why or look for God in the tragedy, look for God in the disappointment or look for God through the sadness. One thing is clear, He has provided us with the tools to navigate, be successful, happy, healthy and prosperous. That does not mean that if you read this book that it offers a magic panacea, but it will provide·you with the toolbox to navigate the difficulties and be victorious.

We have been given so many gifts: a loving family, an education, gainful employment, a home, health, friends and opportunities to change lives and build futures. Through it, we too become disenchanted by the onslaught of challenges and seemingly unrelenting problems and missteps. Yet, He continues to prove to us that WE ARE. Indeed we can be successful as leaders, community members, spouses, parents, friends, college professors, college administrators and general agents of change. Our reach is limitless and limited only by our narrow view of the world and God's reach.

Reading I AM is the best thing you will ever do for yourself or your legacy. Indeed....it is what is needed for a time such as this.

In closing, know what you are not; you are not alone, you are not a failure, you are not unfulfilled, you are not poor in finances or spirit, you are not unkind, , you are not unhealthy, you are not unworthy! You Are...because He deems it so!

Drs. Eric and Armenta Hinton
Susquehanna University
Selinsgrove, Pennsylvania

APOSTLE'S
REFLECTIONS

The publishing of this book excites me because it is one that will enrich kingdom people's lives daily. In February 2012 I was impressed by the Holy Spirit to have the members of the congregation I lead at Spirit of Love Life Empowerment International to re-identify themselves using biblical words or phrases. For example, I am wise, I am redeemed, I am free, I have re –identified myself as: "I am justified by Faith". The authority and assurance that was released in this declaration for me was life changing. I began to experience waves of confidence and spiritual rushes in the revelation of who "I am" in God. "I am" because of His love for me, not because of what I have done or how good I have been or not been, but simply because of how He created me in His image and likeness.

In January 2015, as I was waking the Holy Spirit said write. I reached for my laptop and began to make a list of "I am" statements. There was an anointing so prevalent as I reviewed each statement and I realized the joy our Heavenly Father gets when we agree with what He says about us. I realized that He allows in accordance with what we say. Matthew 12:37 tells us that by our words we are condemned and by our words we are justified. "I Am Declarations & Meditations" will wash over your soul with waves of victory and blow winds of truth about your identity as it relates to the great "I AM".

ACKNOWLEDGMENTS

"I AM..." is a powerful, indispensable manual that will impact and change the lives of many. This book is very well organized and teaches you not only how to meditate but the power of meditation. Apostle Springer was led by the Holy Spirit and produced a masterpiece. "I AM…" allows the reader to recognize the power of their words and be mindful of what they are saying. I have been blessed by this great read and can't wait for the world to have access to it. I recommend this book to anyone that would like to see change manifested in their life.

Prophetess LaKeya Wheaton
Spirit of Love Life Empowerment International
Austell, Georgia

Declaration and meditation are two of the most powerful and immediate means we have at hand to access that secret place in the SPIRIT. Apostle Springer has literally made it so profoundly easy in her book "I AM…Meditations and Declarations".   It is unique in style which makes it easy to find those particular I AMs at your point of need. It is a handbook. Handbooks are well used and well shared. The one-hundred-forty I AMs scripturally presented will certainly cause a person to be drawn into the habit of reaching for this handbook of the Promises of GOD.

Dr. Jacquelyn Ponder, Pastor
In Jesus Name Church Universal, Inc.,
Senoia, Georgia

INTRODUCTION

"LET THE WEAK SAY I AM STRONG"

The essence of this scriptural saying can be used to empower and change your life. "I AM" is a powerful affirmation that can transform life when spoken according to the authority of the Word.

Let the weak say I am strong is found in Joel 3:10. This is God speaking to the prophet Joel and instructing him on how to edify, comfort and exhort His chosen, in particular the tribe of Judah and the people of Jerusalem. Please take note: Judah means praise and Jerusalem was known as the place of worship. These two nations had been in a losing position of captivity and slavery to the Egyptians and saw themselves as weak in comparison to their oppressors. Praise and worship can never be weak. Praise is a lifter of the bowed down head and brings God into your atmosphere, while worship not only exalts God but in so doing, it brings you into his atmosphere. With that being said, how could Judah and the people of Jerusalem (praise & worship) feel or see themselves as weak? We are also guilty of forgetting who we have been identified as.

Scripture teaches us we are fearfully and wonderfully made in His image and likeness, with the ability to do greater works. Yet more than often defeat looms over us and causes feelings of inadequacies. Well the remedy is to proclaim and speak the results you desire. Use the word of the Lord to accomplish victory and change in your life.

Why did God say, "Let the weak say I am strong"? Because God knew what and how He had created them. In verse 9 of Joel 3 He says, "proclaim ye this among the Gentiles; Prepare war, wake up the mighty men, let all the men of war draw near; let them come up." Joel is used to make a public service announcement reminding them of who they were; warriors and mighty men who needed to wake up and fight like men of war. They needed to draw near to God (praise &worship). They needed to come up. You need to come up, get out of that defeated place of weakness and despair. When one experiences disappointment on top of disappointment, on top of disappointment, this births depression. It is my belief that when one is not fulfilling their God given purpose you are bound to wind up repeatedly disappointed and eventually depressed. The biggest battle one faces daily is in the mind. The way you see yourself is the only way God can respond to you in return. The mind has to be transformed not only through the word of God but also through what we say. We must repent for how we have identified ourselves out of the plans and purpose of Gods will.

Hosea 14:2 (Amplified Bible) "Take with you words and return to the Lord. Say to Him, Take away all our iniquity; accept what is good and receive us graciously; so will we render [our thanks] as bullocks [to be sacrificed] and pay the confession of our lips." We must also learn to skillfully plant the right seed of the word that it might prevail in our lives. Acts 19:20 (King James Version) says, " So mightily grew the word of God and prevailed." Yes the seed is the word of God according to Luke 8:11. So what are you saying (planting)?

Joel told the people to wake up to who they were created to be, draw nigh to God and most importantly, even though they felt weak, looked weak and had been demonstrating weakness, to say "I Am Strong." Agree with God say "I Am........................."

1

WHAT'S ON YOUR MIND

*And be not conformed to the things of this world, but be ye
transformed by the renewing of your mind, that you may prove,
what is that good and acceptable and perfect will of God.*

Romans 12:2 KJV

"**I AM**" transformed by the renewing of my mind. What does this really mean? This declaration alone literally has the ability to catapult one's life into heaven on earth, Utopia. Notice I said it has the ability to, not to do, but the ability to. The reason it is ability and not an instant reality is because there is a process involved. The tendency to be conformed to the things of this world is ever present. You must make a conscious effort to avoid the ways and the thinking of the world. Before you can experience heaven on earth there has to be a shifting of your mindset. Mindset is defined as the established set of attitudes held by someone.

Romans 12:2 (MSG) says it this way, *"Do not become so well adjusted to your culture that you fit into it without even thinking. Instead, fix your attention on God, You will be changed from the inside out, readily recognize what he wants from you and respond to it."* Unlike the culture around you always dragging you down to its level of immaturity, God brings the best out of you developing well-formed maturity in you. We are all products of our environment. Where we were born, the neighborhood we grew up in, the time or era in which we were raised, to whom we were born, what spiritual, religious or ministries we have attended, what schools we attended, what friends and family we have been influenced by, all have helped to shape our mindsets. Unfortunately our environment, even spiritual environments have not always been conducive to God's plans for our lives. We have adjusted to and been dragged down to the level of our culture without giving thought to our expected end. Jeremiah 29:11(KJV) says, *"I know the thoughts I think towards you,* says the Lord, *thoughts of peace and not evil, to give you an expected end."* Now it becomes our responsibility to know what God thinks about us and to discover our personal expected end. If God's thoughts and desire for us is peace, perhaps we have not experienced it because of conformation instead of transformation.

II Corinthians 10:5-6 (KJV) says, *"Casting down imaginations and every high thing that exalts itself against the knowledge of God and bringing into captivity every thought to the obedience of Christ; and having in a readiness to revenge all disobedience when your obedience is fulfilled."* Anything that we choose to think, believe, depend upon, trust, adhere to or live by that is contrary to the knowledge of God, must be dealt with severely and revengefully through the process of rejection. To cast down something means to reject it. It means to throw forcefully in a specified direction. The direction is down in this case. God is very specific about things that are exalted against Him. For something to be exalted, it has been lifted up and held high. It holds a powerful position. Take a moment right here and just ask God to reveal to you what things and thoughts you have exalted over Him and His word. Allow me to share a few examples with you to assist in this process.

Often the mindset is so conditioned against the knowledge of the Word of God that we function from two opposing forces. You say *I can't* but the Word says *you can do all things through Christ*. You say *this is too hard*, the Word says *nothing is impossible with God*. You say *I can't live without them* the Word teaches us to choose life. You complain *I just can't get ahead*, while the Word says *the last shall be first*. How often have you decreed *I can't afford that* but scripture teaches that if we seek first His Kingdom and His righteousness, all things will be added to you. God said He will never leave you or forsake you, but you complain about being alone. While many have become content with sickness, *because it runs in the family*, God said I will do a new thing in you. Many of us have legitimized the ungodly character traits or actions in ourselves or others with such statements as:

"*She act just like her great aunt*"
knowing full well great aunt was a bold sinner,

"*He drinks like a fish*"
meaning he is a drunkard,

"*That one is definitely a Jones*"
naturally fat,

"Well, I'm not surprised; high blood pressure does run in the family".

The acceptance of such thinking and practices creates for us and those we speak over a defeated and depressing environment. We have gotten so comfortable with such foolish talking and yet wonder why life is not well with us. How can we have peace and our joy be full when our hearts speak with evil intent? What is so illuminating about this is that the Word says in Titus 2:8 (KJV) *"it is not even convenient to speak filthy, foolish or jesting."* This proves that we have been conformed. We had to be conditioned and trained to adjust to this negative way of thinking in life; for this behavior to have become so easy, it has been practiced, inherited and prioritized. It's been exalted over the knowledge of God.

1 John 5:21 (KJV) says *"little children, keep yourselves from idols."* What is an idol? An image or representation of a God used as an object of worship. What is worship? A feeling or expression of reverence or adoration to a deity; to revere, venerate, adore or exalt.

There are images in our minds of who we are and it is often based on our circumstances and environment. When we fall victim to this image and it does not align itself with the knowledge of God concerning us, we live beneath the peace, success and abundance He promised.

Scriptures referenced in this chapter:
Philippians 4:13; Luke 1:37; Deuteronomy 30:19, 31:6; Matthew 6:33, 20:16; Isaiah 43:19

2

THINKING WITH THE HEART

As a man thinks in his heart, so is he..........
Proverbs 23:7 NIV

We have been conditioned to believe we think with our minds. But the truth is our mind is simply a passage way to our heart. This is why we must cast down imaginations and every high thought exalting itself against the knowledge of God before it reaches our heart. Once a thought reaches the heart it forms, shapes and conditions your life. So in Philippians 2:5-6 (KJV) when we read *"Let this mind be in you which was also in Christ Jesus, who being in the form of God thought it not robbery to be equal with God"*. This is a relevant and noteworthy invitation we should RSVP to. The word *'Let'* here, simply means to allow. Allow your mind to think like Jesus Christ. Allow your mind to receive equality with God. Allow your mind to accept and agree with the fact that you too are made in the image and likeness of God as spoken in Genesis 1:27 (KJV) *"So God created man in His own image, in the image of God created He him, male and female created He them."* Now once you allow this to sink into your heart, from your heart, you too will accept your position with Christ whom you are called into oneness with, according to Galatians 3:28.

The scripture tell us to hide the Word in our hearts that we might not sin against Him. This further clarifies the importance of thinking with our hearts. We do not sin initially from the slipping of our tongues, but as a result of failure to cast down our thoughts and imaginations. We sin when we permit those thoughts to become exalted and grow into our hearts. It is critical that we adhere to Proverbs 4:23 (NIV) *"above all else guard your heart, for everything you do flows from it"*. I'm reminded of a parable Jesus spoke to his disciples in Matthew 21:29. A father goes to his two sons and ask them to go into his vineyard and work. The first son he asked said, "no, I don't want to", but after thinking about it repented and went. The second son said, "yes, I will go", but he did not go. What is in your mind and what is in your heart are not always the same. When your heart is right, in the end, you will do what is right. Our prayer should be *"Create in me a clean heart oh God and renew a right Spirit within me."*

Scriptures referenced in this chapter:
Philippians 2:5-6; Genesis 1:27; Galatians 3:28;
Psalms 51:10, 119:1; Proverbs 4:23; Matthew 21:29

3

SOMETHING TO PROVE

And be not conformed to the things of this world, but be ye transformed by the renewing of your mind, that you may prove, what is that good and acceptable and perfect will of God.

Romans 12:2 KJV

…That you may prove what is that good, perfect and acceptable will of God. God's desire is that His Kingdom comes to the earth. Kingdom people have something to prove to this world. We are not here just passing through. We are here to demonstrate heaven on earth. *Thy Kingdom come, thy will be done in earth as it is in heaven.* The only way this will take place is through the saints of God. We are ambassadors with kingdom citizenship sent here to represent heavenly government. An ambassador is an accredited diplomat sent by a country as an official representative to a foreign country. You never go into a foreign country as an ambassador conforming to the ways of that country. When one does this, he is known as a defector or traitor. When we align ourselves with the ways of this world we become rebels and deserters to our kingdom. This puts us out of the will of God. The bible says in Proverbs 16:7 (KJV) *"When a man's ways please the Lord, he maketh even his enemies to be at peace with him."* Glory to God, even in a world that hates you, you are unstoppable! When we do the will of God we will receive what He has promised. When our lives demonstrate heaven on earth then it brings glory to God. It is our Father's good pleasure to give you the kingdom. When you let your light shine and men see your Godly and good works, it causes others to desire Him. The acceptable and perfect will of God is for man

to be saved. The life you live before your family, friends and enemies is a demonstration of your transformed mind and the thoughts of your heart. It is imperative that what you demonstrate is representing God's Kingdom.

Scriptures referenced in this chapter:
Proverbs 16:7

4

BE

For in Him we live and move and we have our being; of certain also of your own poets have said. For we are also his offspring.

Acts 17:28 KJV

This is a word that has always fascinated me. The definition of *Be* is to equal in meaning and to have same connotation as. *Be* is used to indicate the identity of a person or thing. It is used to indicate the condition of a person or thing. It is used to describe the qualities of a person or thing. Acts17:28 (KJV) *"for in Him we live and move and we have our being; of certain also of your own poets have said. For we are also his offspring."* We can do nothing outside of Him. In order to live the life intended for us, we must perfect our being. In other words we must become complete in all parts, full grown of full age, we must become whole. Our identity, qualities and condition must say we are the seed, the offspring of Christ.

Scriptures referenced in this chapter:
Acts17:28

5
MEDITATION

*Let the words of my mouth and the meditation of my heart, be
acceptable in thy sight, oh Lord my strength and my redeemer
Psalms 19:14*

To meditate is to think deeply or focus ones' mind in silence or with the aid of chanting, for religious or spiritual purposes or as a method of relaxation. So by definition meditation can be performed in two ways. One can engage in meditation:

> 1) By focusing their thoughts in silence or
> 2) By speaking their thoughts out loud

Confession time. I had always been very leery about the terminology of chanting until I had a revelation on Joshua 1:8. It says, *"This book of the law shall not depart out of thy mouth, but thou shalt meditate therein day and night that thou may observe and do according to all that is written therein: for then thou shall make thy way prosperous and then thou shall have good success."(KJV)* 'Shall not depart out of thy mouth' became very alive to me. In all honesty, my ignorance of this phrase embarrassed me because I have always believed in having what you say but the simplicity of saying it as a form of meditation had never clicked. I think the old mindset of what it means to chant and all of the negative and occult connotations of it, has robbed not only me, but many others of its spiritual benefits. To chant simply means a repeated rhythmic phrase. This is what we do every time we sing a song, we chant. Songs of the Lord and prophetic songs are also chants. Demonstrators who march repeating a phrase is a chant. i.e. "No justice no peace."

Ephesians 5:19 (KJV) says *"Speaking to yourselves in psalms and hymns and spiritual songs, singing and making melody in your heart to the Lord."* Let us examine further psalms, hymns and spiritual songs. Well, according to the British Dictionary, Psalms is any of the 150 sacred songs, lyric poems and prayers that together constitute a book, Psalms, of the Old Testament. So there are certain Psalms we should be not only including in our meditations but demonstrate its truths in our daily lives. What a great way to make melody in your heart. A Psalm is actually a piece of music that is accompanied by a voice and an instrument. In biblical times this was usually a harp. Remember David would often play his harp and sing songs to sooth Saul. Following are a few Psalms that remind us of not only who our God is but what He does, who we are and how He feels about us.

Psalm 105:1-15 (KJV)

1 O give thanks unto the LORD; call upon his name: make known his deeds among the people. 2 Sing unto him, sing psalms unto him: talk ye of all his wondrous works. 3 Glory ye in his holy name: let the heart of them rejoice that seek the LORD. 4 Seek the LORD, and his strength: seek his face evermore. 5 Remember his marvelous works that he hath done; his wonders, and the judgments of his mouth; 6 O ye seed of Abraham his servant, ye children of Jacob his chosen. 7 He is the LORD our God: his judgments are in all the earth. 8 He hath remembered his covenant forever, the word which he commanded to a thousand generations. 9 Which covenant he made with Abraham, and his oath unto Isaac; 10 And confirmed the same unto Jacob for a law and to Israel for

an everlasting covenant: 11 Saying, unto thee will I give the land of Canaan, the lot of your inheritance: 12 When they were but a few men in number; yea, very few, and strangers in it. 13 When they went from one nation to another, from one kingdom to another people; 14 He suffered no man to do them wrong: yea, he reproved kings for their sakes; 15 Saying, touch not mine anointed, and do my prophets no harm.

Psalms 113 (KJV)

1 Praise ye the LORD. Praise, O ye servants of the LORD, praise the name of the LORD. 2 Blessed be the name of the LORD from this time forth and for evermore. 3 From the rising of the sun unto the going down of the same the LORD's name is to be praised. 4 The LORD is high above all nations, and his glory above the heavens. 5 Who is like unto the LORD our God, who dwelleth on high, 6 Who humbleth himself to behold the things that are in heaven, and in the earth! 7 He raiseth up the poor out of the dust, and lifteth the needy out of the dunghill; 8 That he may set him with princes, even with the princes of his people. 9 He maketh the barren woman to keep house, and to be a joyful mother of children. Praise ye the LORD.

Psalms 146 (KJV)

1 Praise ye the LORD. Praise the LORD, O my soul. 2 While I live will I praise the LORD: I will sing praises unto my God while I have any being. 3 Put not your trust in princes, nor in the son of man, in whom there is no help. 4 His breath goeth forth, he returneth to his earth; in that very day his thoughts perish. 5 Happy is he that hath the God of Jacob for his help, whose hope is in the LORD his God: 6 Which made heaven, and earth, the sea, and all that therein is: which keepeth truth forever: 7 Which

executeth judgment for the oppressed: which giveth food to the hungry. The LORD looseth the prisoners: 8 The LORD openeth the eyes of the blind: the LORD raiseth them that are bowed down: the LORD loveth the righteous: 9 The LORD preserveth the strangers; he relieveth the fatherless and widow: but the way of the wicked he turneth upside down. 10 The LORD shall reign forever, even thy God, O Zion, unto all generations. Praise ye the LORD.

The Greek word for hymn is *humnos* and is defined as to celebrate or praise. In Ephesians 5:19, a hymn is a spontaneous song not set to music. Once a hymn has been set to music it becomes a psalm. How often have we chanted a hymn, a celebratory rhythmic praise to our God throughout our day originating from a grateful or cheerful heart? Keep making melody in your heart.

Spiritual songs are also known as prophetic songs of the Lord. These are songs that are inspired by the Holy Spirit. The phrase in the Greek is *ode pneumatikos* which is interpreted songs of the breath of God. Inspired by the Holy Spirit, it can be Him speaking to you or through you.

I find it necessary to elaborate on these things because after much consideration, prayer and study I realize how an understanding of the various forms of meditation upon the word will insure Godly and good success. Now as you can see psalms, hymns and spiritual songs do not all mean the same thing. We are instructed to do all three, making melody in our heart. This should further clarify how important and pure the condition of the heart must be and convict one to a more sanctified and dedicated life of transforming to the image of God.

Scriptures referenced in this chapter:
Joshua 1:8; Ephesians 5:19;
Psalm 19:14, 105:1-15, 113, 146

6

HEAL MY RELATIONSHIPS

*For where envying and strife is, there is confusion and
every evil work.*
James 3:16 (KJV)

This section is dedicated specifically to teach on the
importance of harmony in relationships.

Because strife and confusion opens up to every evil
work, it would be futile to empower you with building
tools of success through "I AM" declarations without
appropriately preparing you to maintain that success.
Therefore, it is imperative to evaluate any deep rooted or
hidden areas of strife that can sabotage or destroy your
ability to walk in victory.

Let us look at the definition of strife: Anger or bitter
disagreement over fundamental issues. As you think
about this definition and review the following list, please
be very honest and think about who you are in strife with.
Synonyms for strife include: animosity, argument,
bickering, clash, contradict, controversy, competition,
disunity, disagreement, dysfunction, emulation, fighting,
hassle, quarrel, rivalry, squabble, static, warfare.

In Genesis 13, Abram and Lot discovered that their
herdsmen were not getting along and Abram said to Lot
verse 18 *"Let there be no strife, I pray thee, between me
and thee and between my herdsmen and thy herdsmen:
for we be brethren"(KJV)*. Abram called a truce; he
peacefully confronted the problem and humbled himself

by suggesting Lot choose the land he wanted to occupy first. After Lot made his decision on which direction he would go, Abram did not argue with him, he trusted God. The land Lot chose was well watered and the best choice conducive to both of their occupations. Once Abram called a truce and separated himself from strife, God told him he would give him as far as he could see and bless his seed. Proverbs 28:25 (KJV) states *"He that is of a proud heart stir up strife: but he that put his trust in the Lord shall be made fat."*

Proverbs 17:1 says *"Better is a dry morsel and quietness therewith, than a house full of sacrifices with strife"(KJV).* In other words all of your spiritual sacrifices for success are useless in the eyes of God if you have strife in your house. You will be better off in the sight of God to have little to nothing to sustain your existence. Think about this. God always has your best interest at heart, so now the question becomes are you able to handle, without strife, what He desires to release in your life. As I meditate on this, I realize the reality of *this* truth. Struggle humbles…when a person is struggling there is really no time for strife, although it may be present, it is minimized because the focus is on survival and the achievement of something important. People tend to come together and put aside or call a truce to their differences for the sake of accomplishing a mutual goal. My interpretation of Proverbs 17:1 is that strife is like water that has been leaked out, you cannot gather it back.

Before proceeding any further please conduct the following exercises to uproot strife. Pray this prayer: *Father, forgive me for operating in strife. I recognize that it is rooted in pride, anger, self- exaltation and even rebellion. Reveal to me areas of strife, confusion and evil works in my life that I may surrender it to you. I ask that you release to me all that you have for me and that Holy Spirit convicts me when and where needed, that I may be able to maintain your blessings with no sorrow added in Jesus name.*

Anonyms for Strife: Accord, agreement, concurrence, calm, conformity, harmony, peace, success, truce, unity and victory.

Scriptures referenced in this chapter:
Genesis 13:16; Proverbs 17:1, 28:2

7

TRANSFORM YOUR MIND, TRANSFORM YOUR LIFE

*But his delight in is the law of the Lord and in his law
doth he meditate day and night, And he shall be like a
tree planted by the rivers of water that bring forth his
fruit in his season; His leaf also shall not wither; and
whatsoever he doth shall prosper.*
Psalm 1:2 (KJV)

Just as we have practiced, inherited, prioritized by
default or intentionally, the wrong and negative foolish
jesting, we must now condition our mind and heart to
align itself with the knowledge of God's Word. We must
adhere to the power of success through obedience to
meditation in the Word of God. Philippians 4:7 (KJV)
states, *"And the peace of God, which passes all
understanding, shall keep your hearts and minds through
Christ Jesus. Finally, brethren, whatsoever things are
true, whatsoever things are honest, whatsoever things are
just, whatsoever things are pure, whatsoever things are
lovely, whatsoever things are of good report; if there be
any virtue and if there be any praise, think on these
things."*

Why "I Am"

There is a song we sing based on Romans 8:27 that
says *"I am what God says I am, I am what God says I am
, I'm more than a conqueror through Him that love me, I
am what God says I am."* This song or chant is a good

one to meditate upon. To be a conqueror is great but to be more than a conqueror means that your adversary is inexplicably no match for you. Just as the fire was no match for the three Hebrew boys and the lions were no match for Daniel, you also are more than a conqueror. It is from this bold place of confidence you must forge forward in life to pursue and achieve everything God has for you. Like Paul, when bitten by serpents, shake it off! Like the Shunammite woman when faced with death of a promise, decree it is well. The ability of God lies within and has to be called forth and awakened. Believe **I am what God says I am!**

The word according to Joel 3:10, *"Beat your plow sheds into swords and your pruning hooks into spears, let the weak say **I am** strong (KJV)."* It does not matter what a situation appears to be, we must literally say what or who we are based on the truth of the word of God. *Calling those things that be not as though they were* (Romans 4:17). We have been given many precious promises and the only thing that is denying us access is not experiencing the full knowledge of God and accepting who we are.

Because faith comes by hearing, we must declare and not just meditate. The "I AM" declarations and meditations in this book are accompanied by foundational scriptures that will support the upgrading of your mind and heart, developing and transforming it to a mindset that agrees with the great *"I Am that I Am."*

Scriptures referenced in this chapter:
Philippians 4:7; Romans 4:17, 8:27; Joel 3:10

8

DECLARATIONS & MEDITATIONS

I AM WHO GOD SAYS I AM

Colossians 3:9-10 (KJV)

9 Lie not one to another, seeing that ye have put off the old man with his deeds; 10 And have put on the new man, which is renewed in knowledge after the image of him that created him:

Philippians 3:20-21 (MSG)

But there's far more to life for us. We're citizens of high heaven! We're waiting the arrival of the Savior, the Master, Jesus Christ, who will transform our earthy bodies into glorious bodies like his own. He'll make us beautiful and whole with the same powerful skill by which he is putting everything as it should be, under and around him.

I AM FREE TO BE ME

Genesis 5:1-2 (MSG)

This is the family tree of the human race: When God created the human race, he made it godlike, with a nature akin to God. He created both male and female and blessed them, the whole human race.

Romans 8:2 (KJV)

For the law of the Spirit of life in Christ Jesus hath made me free from the law of sin and death

I AM FORGIVEN

1 John 1:9 (KJV)
If we confess our sins, He is faithful and just to forgive us our sins and to cleanse us from all unrighteousness.

I AM FORGIVING

Matthew 6:14-15 (KJV)
14 For if ye forgive men their trespasses, your heavenly Father will also forgive you: 15 But if ye forgive not men their trespasses, neither will your Father forgive your trespasses.

Colossians 3:13 (KJV)
Forbearing one another and forgiving one another, if any man have a quarrel against any: even as Christ forgave you, so also do ye.

I AM LIVING BY FAITH

2 Corinthians 5:7 (KJV)
For we walk by faith, not by sight

2 Corinthians 5:6-8 (MSG)
That's why we live with such good cheer. You won't see us drooping our heads or dragging our feet! Cramped conditions here don't get us down. They only remind us of the spacious living conditions ahead. It's what we trust in but don't yet see that keeps us going. Do you suppose a few ruts in the road or rocks in the path are going to stop us? When the time comes, we'll be plenty ready to exchange exile for homecoming.

I AM RIGHTEOUS

Romans 5:17 (GNT)

It is true that through the sin of one man death began to rule because of that one man. But how much greater is the result of what was done by the one man, Jesus Christ! All who receive God's abundant grace and are freely put right with him will rule in life through Christ.

I AM A CHILD OF THE HIGHEST GOD

1 Peter 1:23 (KJV)

Being born again, not of corruptible seed but of incorruptible, by the word of God, which live and abides forever.

(Name something in your life that you thought would overtake you, but your heavenly father brought you out of.)

I AM A FRIEND OF GOD

John 15:14 (KJV)

Ye are my friends, if ye do whatsoever I command you.

I AM FEARFULLY AND WONDERFULLY MADE

Psalm 139:14 (KJV)

I will praise thee; for I am fearfully and wonderfully made: marvelous are thy works; and that my soul knows right well.

I AM FIRST

Matthew 19:28-30 (MSG)

Jesus replied, "Yes, you have followed me. In the re-creation of the world, when the Son of Man will rule gloriously, you who have followed me will also rule, starting with the twelve tribes of Israel. And not only you, but anyone who sacrifices home, family, fields—whatever—because of me will get it all back a hundred times over, not to mention the considerable bonus of eternal life. This is the Great Reversal: many of the first ending up last, and the last first."

I AM ABOVE

Philippians 2:15 (KJV)

That ye may be blameless and harmless, the Sons of God, without rebuke, in the midst of a crooked and perverse nation, among whom ye shine as lights in the world.

I AM LIGHT

Matthew 5:14 (KJV)

Ye are the light of the world. A city that is set on a hill cannot be hid.

I AM BORN OF THE SPIRIT

John 3:5 (KJV)

Jesus answered, Verily, verily, I say unto thee, except a man be born of water and of the Spirit, He cannot enter into the kingdom of God.

I AM DRAWING NIGH TO GOD

James 4:8 (KJV)
Draw nigh to God and he will draw nigh to you. Cleanse your hands, ye sinners; and purify your hearts, ye double minded.

I AM DILIGENT

Proverbs 22:29 (KJV)
Seest thou a man diligent in his business? He shall stand before kings; he shall not stand before mean men.

Hebrews 11:6 (KJV)
But without faith it is impossible to please him: for he that cometh to God must believe that he is, and that he is a rewarder of them that diligently seek him.

I AM SEALED BY THE HOLY SPIRIT

Ephesians 1:13 (KJV)
In whom ye also trusted, after that ye heard the word of truth, the gospel of your salvation: in whom also after that ye believed, ye were sealed with that Holy Spirit of promise.

Ephesians 4:30 (KJV)
And grieve not the Holy Spirit of God, whereby ye are sealed unto the day of redemption.

I AM SENSITIVE TO THE HOLY SPIRIT

2 Corinthians 1:22 (KJV)
Who hath also sealed us and given the earnest of the Spirit in our hearts.

John 8:47 (GW)

The person who belongs to God understands what God says. You don't understand because you don't belong to God.

I AM COMMUNING WITH GOD

Job 22:21-25 (MSG)

Give in to God, come to terms with him and everything will turn out just fine. Let him tell you what to do; take his words to heart. Come back to God Almighty and he'll rebuild your life. Clean house of everything evil. Relax your grip on your money and abandon your gold-plated luxury. God Almighty will be your treasure, more wealth than you can imagine.

I AM DEAD TO SIN

Romans 6:11 (KJV)

Likewise reckon ye also yourselves to be dead indeed unto sin, but alive unto God through Jesus Christ our Lord.

I AM REDEEMED

Ephesians 1:7 (KJV)

In whom we have redemption through his blood, the forgiveness of sins, according to the riches of his grace.

Galatians 3:13 (KJV)

Christ hath redeemed us from the curse of the law, being made a curse for us: for it is written, Cursed is every one that hangs on a tree.

I AM SEATED IN HEAVENLY PLACES

Ephesians 2:6-7 (KJV)

6 And hath raised us up together, and made us sit together in heavenly places in Christ Jesus: 7 That in the ages to come he might shew the exceeding riches of his grace in his kindness toward us through Christ Jesus.

I AM LIVING IN FULLNESS OF JOY

Psalm 16:11 (KJV)

Thou wilt shew me the path of life: in thy presence is fullness of joy; at thy right hand there are pleasures for evermore.

I AM WISE

1 Corinthians 2:16 (KJV)

For who hath known the mind of the Lord, that he may instruct him? But we have the mind of Christ.

1 Kings 3:9-12 (KJV)

9 Give therefore thy servant an understanding heart to judge thy people that I may discern between good and bad: for who is able to judge this thy so great a people? 10 And the speech pleased the LORD, that Solomon had asked this thing. 11 And God said unto him, Because thou hast asked this thing, and hast not asked for thyself long life; neither hast asked riches for thyself, nor hast asked the life of thine enemies; but hast asked for thyself understanding to discern judgment; 12 Behold, I have done according to thy words: lo, I have given thee a wise and an understanding heart; so that there was none like thee before thee, neither after thee shall any arise like unto thee

I AM SEEKING GOD WITH ALL OF MY HEART

2 Chronicles 31:21 (KJV)

And in every work that he began in the service of the house of God, and in the law and in the commandments, to seek his God, he did it with all his heart and prospered.

I AM A BRANCH OF THE TRUE VINE

John 15:1 (KJV)

I am the true vine and my Father is the husbandman.

John 15:5 (KJV)

I am the vine, ye are the branches: He that abideth in me and I in Him, the same bringeth forth much fruit: for without me ye can do nothing.

I AM BEARING FRUIT THAT REMAINS

John 15:16 (KJV)

Ye have not chosen me but I have chosen you and ordained you, that ye should go and bring forth fruit and that your fruit should remain: that whatsoever ye shall ask of the Father in my name, he may give it you.

I AM TRANSFORMED BY THE RENEWING OF MY MIND

Romans 12:2 (KJV)

And be not conformed to this world: but be ye transformed by the renewing of your mind, that ye may prove what is that good and acceptable and perfect, will of God.

I AM THANKFUL

Colossians 2:6-7 (KJV)

6 As ye have therefore received Christ Jesus the Lord, so walk ye in him: 7 Rooted and built up in Him and stablished in the faith, as ye have been taught, abounding therein with thanksgiving.

I AM FULL OF FAITH

2 Corinthians 4:13-14 (KJV)

13 We having the same spirit of faith, according as it is written, I believed and therefore have I spoken; we also believe and therefore speak; 14 Knowing that he which raised up the Lord Jesus shall raise up us also by Jesus, and shall present us with you.

I AM DELIVERED BEFORE I EXPERIENCE LABOR PAINS

Isaiah 66:7-9 (KJV)

7 Before she travailed, she brought forth; before her pain came, she was delivered of a man child. 8 Who hath heard such a thing? Who hath seen such things? Shall the earth be made to bring forth in one day? Shall a nation be born at once? For as soon as Zion travailed, she brought forth her children. 9 Shall I bring to the birth and not cause to bring forth? Saith the LORD: shall I cause to bring forth and shut the womb? Saith thy God.

I AM DWELLING IN THE SECRET PLACE

Psalm 91 (KJV)

1 He that dwelleth in the secret place of the most High shall abide under the shadow of the Almighty. 2 I will say

of the LORD, He is my refuge and my fortress: my God; in him will I trust. 3 Surely he shall deliver thee from the snare of the fowler and from the noisome pestilence. 4 He shall cover thee with his feathers and under his wings shalt thou trust: his truth shall be thy shield and buckler. 5 Thou shalt not be afraid for the terror by night; nor for the arrow that flieth by day 6 Nor for the pestilence that walketh in darkness; nor for the destruction that wasteth at noonday. 7 A thousand shall fall at thy side, and ten thousand at thy right hand; but it shall not come nigh thee. 8 Only with thine eyes shalt thou behold and see the reward of the wicked. 9 Because thou hast made the LORD, which is my refuge, even the most High, thy habitation; 10 There shall no evil befall thee, neither shall any plague come nigh thy dwelling. 11 For he shall give His angels charge over thee, to keep thee in all thy ways. 12 They shall bear thee up in their hands, lest thou dash thy foot against a stone. 13 Thou shalt tread upon the lion and adder: the young lion and the dragon shalt thou trample under feet. 14 Because He hath set his love upon me, therefore will I deliver him: I will set him on high, because he hath known my name. 15 He shall call upon me, and I will answer him: I will be with Him in trouble; I will deliver Him, and honor Him. 16 With long life will I satisfy Him and shew Him my salvation.

I AM CARING

1 Peter 4:7-11 (MSG)

Everything in the world is about to be wrapped up, so take nothing for granted. Stay wide-awake in prayer. Most of all, love each other as if your life depended on it. Love makes up for practically anything. Be quick to give a meal to the hungry, a bed to the homeless—cheerfully. Be generous with the different things God gave you, passing them around so all get in on it: if words, let it be God's words; if help, let it be God's hearty help. That way, God's bright presence will be evident in everything through Jesus, and he'll get all the credit as the One mighty in everything—encores to the end of time. Oh, yes!

I AM EXPERIENCING GODS GRACE

Ephesians 2:8-9 (KJV)

8 For by grace are ye saved through faith; and that not of yourselves: it is the gift of God: 9 Not of works, lest any man should boast.

I AM JUSTIFIED

Romans 3:24 (KJV)

Being justified freely by his grace through the redemption that is in Christ Jesus.

I AM LIVING IN PEACE

Philippians 4:7 (KJV)

And the peace of God, which passeth all understanding, shall keep your hearts and minds through Christ Jesus.

I AM CONTENT

Hebrews 13:5 (KJV)

Let your conversation be without covetousness; and be content with such things as ye have: for he hath said, I will never leave thee, nor forsake thee.

I AM SUPPLIED ALL MY NEEDS

Philippians 4:19 (KJV)
But my God shall supply all your need according to his riches in glory by Christ Jesus.

I AM DOING GOOD WORKS

Ephesians 2:10 (KJV)
For we are his workmanship, created in Christ Jesus unto good works, which God hath before ordained that we should walk in them.

I AM SANCTIFIED

John 17:16-17 (KJV)
16 They are not of the world, even as I am not of the world. 17 Sanctify them through thy truth: thy word is truth.

I AM AN INTERCESSOR

1 Timothy 2:1-4 (KJV)
1 I exhort therefore, that, first of all, supplications, prayers, intercessions and giving of thanks, be made for all men; 2 For kings, and for all that are in authority; that we may lead a quiet and peaceable life in all godliness and honesty. 3 For this is good and acceptable in the sight of God our Saviour; 4 Who will have all men to be saved and to come unto the knowledge of the truth.

I AM THE SOLUTION

2 Peter 1:3-4 (MSG)

Everything that goes into a life of pleasing God has been miraculously given to us by getting to know, personally and intimately, the One who invited us to God. The best invitation we ever received! We were also given absolutely terrific promises to pass on to you—your tickets to participation in the life of God after you turned your back on a world corrupted by lust.

I AM BOLD

Proverbs 28:1 (KJV)

The wicked flee when no man pursueth: but the righteous are bold as a lion.

I AM CHOSEN

1 Peter 2:9 (KJV)

But ye are a chosen generation, a royal priesthood, an holy nation, a peculiar people; that ye should shew forth the praises of him who hath called you out of darkness into his marvelous light.

I AM RICH

Psalm 112:2-3 (KJV)

2 His seed shall be mighty upon earth: the generation of the upright shall be blessed. 3 Wealth and riches shall be in his house: and his righteousness endureth forever.

I AM CONFIDENT

1 John 5:14-15 (KJV)
14 And this is the confidence that we have in him, that, if we ask any thing according to his will, he heareth us: 15 And if we know that he hear us, whatsoever we ask, we know that we have the petitions that we desired of him.

I AM RECEIVING THINGS

Matthew 6:33 (KJV)
But seek ye first the kingdom of God and his righteousness; and all these things shall be added unto you.

Ephesians 1:13-14 (MSG)
It's in Christ that you, once you heard the truth and believed it (this Message of your salvation), found yourselves home free—signed, sealed and delivered by the Holy Spirit. This signet from God is the first installment on what's coming, a reminder that we'll get everything God has planned for us, a praising and glorious life.

I AM PHYSICALLY FIT

1 Corinthians 6:19 (KJV)
What? know ye not that your body is the temple of the Holy Ghost which is in you, which ye have of God and ye are not your own?

Proverbs 3:7-8 (KJV)
7 Be not wise in thine own eyes: fear the LORD and depart from evil. 8 It shall be health to thy navel and marrow to thy bones.

I AM A CHEERFUL GIVER

2 Corinthians 9:6-11 (KJV)
6 But this I say, He which soweth sparingly shall reap also sparingly; and he which soweth bountifully shall reap also bountifully. 7 Every man according as He purposeth in his heart, so let him give; not grudgingly, or of necessity: for God loveth a cheerful giver. 8 And God is able to make all grace abound toward you; that ye, always having all sufficiency in all things, may abound to every good work: 9 As it is written, He hath dispersed abroad; he hath given to the poor: his righteousness remaineth forever. 10 Now he that ministereth seed to the sower both minister bread for your food and multiply your seed sown and increase the fruits of your righteousness; 11 Being enriched in everything to all bountifulness, which causeth through us thanksgiving to God.

I AM SUBDUING THE EARTH

Genesis 1:28 (KJV)
And God blessed them and God said unto them, Be fruitful and multiply and replenish the earth and subdue it: and have dominion over the fish of the sea and over the fowl of the air and over every living thing that moveth upon the earth.

I AM ANOINTED

2 Corinthians 1:21 (KJV)
Now he which stablisheth us with you in Christ and hath anointed us, is God;

I AM A LIBERAL SOUL

Proverbs 11:25 (KJV)
The liberal soul shall be made fat: and he that watereth shall be watered also himself.

I AM A REVELATOR

Ephesians 1:17 (KJV)
That the God of our Lord Jesus Christ, the Father of glory, may give unto you the spirit of wisdom and revelation in the knowledge of him:

I AM AN ILLUMINATOR

Colossians 1:26 (KJV)
Even the mystery which hath been hid from ages and from generations, but now is made manifest to his saints

I AM AN INSPIRATION

1 Thessalonians 5:11 (ESV)
Therefore encourage one another and build one another up, just as you are doing.

I AM OBEDIENT

Deuteronomy 30:19-20 (KJV)
19 I call heaven and earth to record this day against you, that I have set before you life and death, blessing and cursing: therefore choose life, that both thou and thy seed may live: 20 That thou mayest love the LORD thy God, and that thou mayest obey his voice and that thou mayest cleave unto him: for he is thy life and the length of thy days: that thou mayest dwell in the land which the LORD

sware unto thy fathers, to Abraham, to Isaac and to Jacob, to give them.

I AM STUDYING HIS WORD

2 Timothy 2:15 (KJV)
Study to shew thyself approved unto God, a workman that needeth not to be ashamed, rightly dividing the word of truth.

I AM FOCUSED

2 Chronicles 26:5 (KJV)
And he sought God in the days of Zechariah, who had understanding in the visions of God: and as long as he sought the LORD, God made him to prosper.

I AM DETERMINED

1 Corinthians 15:58 (KJV)
Therefore, my beloved brethren, be ye stedfast, unmoveable, always abounding in the work of the Lord, forasmuch as ye know that your labour is not in vain in the Lord.

I AM GIVEN OPPORTUNITIES

Galatians 6:10 (KJV)
As we have therefore opportunity, let us do good unto all men, especially unto them who are of the household of faith.

I AM UNSTOPPABLE

1 John 4:4 (KJV)
Ye are of God, little children and have overcome them: because greater is he that is in you, than he that is in the world.

I AM ACCOMPLISHED

Philippians 4:13 (KJV)
I can do all things through Christ which strengthened me.

I AM VICTORIOUS

1 Corinthians 15:57 (KJV)
But thanks be to God, which giveth us the victory through our Lord Jesus Christ.

I AM A GOOD STEWARD

1 Peter 4:10 (KJV)
As every man hath received the gift, even so minister the same one to another, as good stewards of the manifold grace of God.

I AM TEACHABLE

Deuteronomy 6:1-3 (KJV)
1 Now these are the commandments, the statutes and the judgments, which the LORD your God commanded to teach you, that ye might do them in the land whither ye go to possess it: 2 That thou might fear the LORD thy God, to keep all his statutes and his commandments, which I command thee, thou and thy son and thy son's

son, all the days of thy life; and that thy days may be prolonged. 3 Hear therefore, O Israel and observe to do it; that it may be well with thee and that ye may increase mightily, as the LORD God of thy fathers hath promised thee, in the land that flow with milk and honey.

I AM TAUGHT OF THE HOLY SPIRIT

Luke 12:12 (KJV)
For the Holy Ghost shall teach you in the same hour what ye ought to say.

I AM WEALTHY

Proverbs 8:18-21 (KJV)
18 Riches and honor are with me; yea, durable riches and righteousness. 19 My fruit is better than gold, yea, than fine gold; and my revenue than choice silver. 20 I lead in the way of righteousness, in the midst of the paths of judgment: 21 That I may cause those that love me to inherit substance; and I will fill their treasures.

I AM BLAMELESS

1 Thessalonians 5:23 (KJV)
And the very God of peace sanctify you wholly; and I pray God your whole spirit and soul and body be preserved blameless unto the coming of our Lord Jesus Christ

I AM POWERFUL

Mark 16:17-18 (KJV)
17 And these signs shall follow them that believe; In my name shall they cast out devils; they shall speak with

new tongues; 18 They shall take up serpents; and if they drink any deadly thing, it shall not hurt them; they shall lay hands on the sick, and they shall recover.

I AM DEMONSTRATING SPECIAL MIRACLES

Acts 19:11 (KJV)
And God wrought special miracles by the hands of Paul.

I AM OPERATING IN LOVE

Ephesians 4:31-32 (KJV)
31 Let all bitterness and wrath and anger and clamour and evil speaking, be put away from you, with all malice: 32 And be ye kind one to another, tenderhearted, forgiving one another, even as God for Christ's sake hath forgiven you.

I AM EXPERIENCING THE LOVE OF GOD

Romans 5:8 (KJV)
But God commendeth his love toward us, in that, while we were yet sinners, Christ died for us.

I AM HEALED

Isaiah 53:5 (KJV)
But he was wounded for our transgressions, he was bruised for our iniquities: the chastisement of our peace was upon him; and with his stripes we are healed.

I AM EMOTIONALLY HEALED

Psalm 147:3 (KJV)
He healeth the broken in heart and bindeth up their

wounds.

I AM RELATIONALLY HEALED

Isaiah 41:10 (GW)
Don't be afraid, because I am with you. Don't be intimidated; I am your God. I will strengthen you. I will help you. I will support you with my victorious right hand.

I AM SPIRITUALLY HEALED

2 Corinthians 5:17 (KJV)
Therefore if any man be in Christ, he is a new creature: old things are passed away; behold, all things are become new.

I AM GENERATIONALLY BLESSED

Daniel 4:3(KJV)
How great are His signs! and how mighty are His wonders! His kingdom is an everlasting kingdom and His dominion is from generation to generation.

I AM PHYSICALLY HEALED

John 11:4 (KJV)
When Jesus heard that, he said, This sickness is not unto death, but for the glory of God, that the Son of God might be glorified thereby.

Psalm 103:3 (KJV)
Who forgiveth all thine iniquities; who healeth all thy diseases;

I AM HEALED SKELETALLY

Proverbs 17:22 (KJV)
A merry heart doeth good like a medicine: but a broken spirit drieth the bones.

I AM RELEASING RIVERS OF LIVING WATERS

John 7:38 (KJV)
He that believeth on me, as the scripture hath said, out of his belly shall flow rivers of living water.

I AM HUMBLE

James 4:10 (KJV)
Humble yourselves in the sight of the Lord and he shall lift you up.

I AM BEGOTTEN OF GOD

1 John 5:18 (KJV)
We know that whosoever is born of God sinneth not; but he that is begotten of God keepeth himself and that wicked one toucheth him not.

I AM AN AMBASSADOR FOR CHRIST

2 Corinthians 5:20 (KJV)
Now then we are ambassadors for Christ, as though God did beseech you by us: we pray you in Christ's stead, be ye reconciled to God

I AM A THREAT TO THE ENEMY

Psalm 143:12 (KJV)
And of thy mercy cut off mine enemies and destroy all them that afflict my soul: for I am thy servant.

I AM A DISCIPLE

John 15:8 (KJV)
Herein is my Father glorified, that ye bear much fruit; so shall ye be my disciples.

I AM A WATERED GARDEN

Isaiah 58:10-11 (KJV)
10 And if thou draw out thy soul to the hungry and satisfy the afflicted soul; then shall thy light rise in obscurity and thy darkness be as the noon day: 11 And the LORD shall guide thee continually and satisfy thy soul in drought and make fat thy bones: and thou shalt be like a watered garden and like a spring of water, whose waters fail not.

I AM BLESSED

Ecclesiastes 5:19 (KJV)
Every man also to whom God hath given riches and wealth and hath given him power to eat thereof and to take his portion and to rejoice in his labour; this is the gift of God.

I AM ACKNOWLEDGING HIM

Proverbs 3:6 (KJV)

In all thy ways acknowledge him and he shall direct thy paths.

I AM FOLLOWING THE GOOD SHEPHERD

Psalm 23 (KJV)

1 The LORD is my shepherd; I shall not want. 2 He maketh me to lie down in green pastures: he leadeth me beside the still waters. 3 He restoreth my soul: he leadeth me in the paths of righteousness for his name's sake. 4 Yea, though I walk through the valley of the shadow of death, I will fear no evil: for thou art with me; thy rod and thy staff they comfort me. 5 Thou preparest a table before me in the presence of mine enemies: thou anointest my head with oil; my cup runneth over. 6 Surely goodness and mercy shall follow me all the days of my life: and I will dwell in the house of the LORD forever.

I AM FOUND (WOMEN)

Proverbs 18:22 (KJV)

Whoso findeth a wife findeth a good thing and obtaineth favour of the LORD.

I AM OBTAINING FAVOR (MEN)

Proverbs 18:22 (KJV)

Whoso findeth a wife findeth a good thing and obtaineth favour of the LORD.

I AM A WORSHIPPER

John 4:24 (KJV)
God is a Spirit: and they that worship him must worship him in spirit and in truth.

I AM FAVORED BY GOD AND MAN

Psalm 102:13 (GW)
You will rise and have compassion on Zion, because it is time to grant a favor to it. Indeed, the appointed time has come.

I AM SUCCESSFUL

Romans 8:28 (KJV)
And we know that all things work together for good to them that love God, to them who are the called according to his purpose.

I AM LIVING LIFE MORE ABUNDANTLY

John 10:10 (KJV)
The thief cometh not, but for to steal and to kill and to destroy: I am come that they might have life and that they might have it more abundantly.

I AM LIVING IN THE OVERFLOW

2 Corinthians 9:8-10 (KJV)
8 And God is able to make all grace abound toward you; that ye, always having all sufficiency in all things, may abound to every good work: 9 (As it is written, He hath dispersed abroad; he hath given to the poor: his righteousness remains forever. 10 Now he that ministers

seed to the sower both minister bread for your food and multiplies your seed sown and increase the fruit of your righteousness:

I AM RESOURCEFUL

John 6:12 (KJV)
When they were filled, he said unto his disciples, Gather up the fragments that remain, that nothing be lost.

I AM IN RIGHT RELATIONSHIPS

Proverbs 13:20 (KJV)
He that walks with wise men shall be wise: but a companion of fools shall be destroyed.

I AM LIVING A BALANCED LIFE

Ecclesiastes 7:16 (KJV)
Be not righteous over much; neither make thyself over wise: why should thou destroy thyself?

Proverbs 11:1 (KJV)
A false balance is abomination to the LORD: but a just weight is his delight.

I AM FREE OF BONDAGES

2 Corinthians 3:17 (KJV)
Now the Lord is that Spirit: and where the Spirit of the Lord is, there is liberty.

I AM ADVANCING IN THE WISDOM OF GOD

James 1:5 (KJV)
If any of you lack wisdom, let him ask of God, that giveth to all men liberally and upbraideth not; and it shall be given him.

I AM DEBT FREE

Romans 13:7-8 (KJV)
7 Render therefore to all their dues: tribute to whom tribute is due; custom to whom custom; fear to whom fear; honor to whom honor. 8 Owe no man anything, but to love one another: for he that loveth another hath fulfilled the law.

I AM COMPLETE

Colossians 2:10-12 (KJV)
10 And ye are complete in him, which is the head of all principality and power: 11 In whom also ye are circumcised with the circumcision made without hands, in putting off the body of the sins of the flesh by the circumcision of Christ: 12 Buried with him in baptism, wherein also ye are risen with him through the faith of the operation of God, who hath raised him from the dead.

I AM DESTINED

Jeremiah 29:11 (KJV)
For I know the thoughts that I think toward you, saith the LORD, thoughts of peace, and not of evil, to give you an expected end.

I AM LIVING IN PURPOSE

Jeremiah 1:5 (KJV)
Before I formed thee in the belly I knew thee; and before thou came forth out of the womb I sanctified thee and I ordained thee a prophet unto the nations

I AM SPIRITUALLY CORRECT

1 Peter 2:5 (KJV)
Ye also, as lively stones, are built up a spiritual house, an holy priesthood, to offer up spiritual sacrifices, acceptable to God by Jesus Christ.

I AM STRONG

Colossians 1:11 (KJV)
Strengthened with all might, according to his glorious power, unto all patience and longsuffering with joyfulness;

I AM SETTING PROPER BOUNDARIES

Colossians 4:6 (KJV)
Let your speech be always with grace, seasoned with salt, that ye may know how ye ought to answer every man.

Galatians 6:5 (KJV)
For every man shall bear his own burden.

I AM BEING PERFECTED

Psalm 138:8 (KJV)
The LORD will perfect that which concerneth me: thy mercy, O LORD, endureth forever: forsake not the works of thine own hands.

I AM AN ATMOSPHERE CHANGER

Ezekiel 37:1-10 (KJV)
1 The hand of the LORD was upon me and carried me out in the spirit of the LORD and set me down in the midst of the valley which was full of bones 2 And caused me to pass by them round about: and, behold, there were very many in the open valley; and lo, they were very dry. 3 And he said unto me, Son of man, can these bones live? And I answered, O Lord GOD, thou knowest. 4 Again he said unto me, Prophesy upon these bones and say unto them, O ye dry bones, hear the word of the LORD. 5 Thus saith the Lord GOD unto these bones; Behold, I will cause breath to enter into you and ye shall live: 6 And I will lay sinews upon you and will bring up flesh upon you, and cover you with skin and put breath in you and ye shall live; and ye shall know that I am the LORD. 7 So I prophesied as I was commanded: and as I prophesied, there was a noise and behold a shaking and the bones came together, bone to his bone. 8 And when I beheld, lo, the sinews and the flesh came up upon them and the skin covered them above: but there was no breath in them. 9 Then said he unto me, Prophesy unto the wind, prophesy, son of man and say to the wind, Thus saith the Lord GOD; Come from the four winds, O breath and breathe upon these slain, that they may live. 10 So I prophesied as he commanded me and the breath came into them and they lived and stood up upon their feet, an exceeding

great army.

I AM KIND

Colossians 3:12 (KJV)
Put on therefore, as the elect of God, holy and beloved, bowels of mercies, kindness, humbleness of mind, meekness, longsuffering;

I AM WALKING IN MY CALLING

Ephesians 4:1 (KJV)
I therefore, the prisoner of the Lord, beseech you that ye walk worthy of the vocation wherewith ye are called.

I AM CLEANSED THROUGH THE BLOOD

1 John 1:7 (KJV)
But if we walk in the light, as he is in the light, we have fellowship one with another and the blood of Jesus Christ his Son cleanse us from all sin.

I AM ORGANIZED

1 Corinthians 14:40 (KJV)
Let all things be done decently and in order.

I AM ADMINISTRATIVE

1 Timothy 3:4-5 (KJV)
4 One that rules well his own house, having his children in subjection with all gravity; 5 For if a man know not how to rule his own house, how shall he take care of the church of God?

I AM ESTABLISHING A SPIRITUAL LEGACY

Joel 1:3 (KJV)
Tell ye your children of it and let your children tell their children and their children another generation.

I AM A SUCCESSFUL INVESTOR

Jeremiah 17:7-8 (KJV)
7 Blessed is the man that trusteth in the LORD and whose hope the LORD is. 8 For he shall be as a tree planted by the waters and that spreadeth out her roots by the river and shall not see when heat cometh, but her leaf shall be green; and shall not be careful in the year of drought, neither shall cease from yielding fruit.

Ecclesiastes 11:1-2 (KJV)
1 Cast thy bread upon the waters: for thou shalt find it after many days 2 Give a portion to seven and also to eight; for thou knowest not what evil shall be upon the earth.

Luke 19:15-17 (KJV)
15 And it came to pass, that when he was returned, having received the kingdom, then he commanded these servants to be called unto him, to whom he had given the money, that he might know how much every man had gained by trading. 16 Then came the first, saying, Lord, thy pound hath gained ten pounds. 17 And he said unto him, Well, thou good servant: because thou hast been faithful in a very little, have thou authority over ten cities.

I AM SOWING AND REAPING AT THE SAME TIME

Amos 9:13 (MSG)
"Yes indeed, it won't be long now." God's Decree.
"Things are going to happen so fast your head will swim, one thing fast on the heels of the other. You won't be able to keep up. Everything will be happening at once—and everywhere you look, blessings! Blessings like wine pouring off the mountains and hills. I'll make everything right again for my people Israel: They'll rebuild their ruined cities. They'll plant vineyards and drink good wine. They'll work their gardens and eat fresh vegetables. And I'll plant them, plant them on their own land. They'll never again be uprooted from the land I've given them. GOD, your God, says so.

I AM LEAVING AN INHERITANCE FOR MY CHILDREN'S CHILDREN

Proverbs 13:22 (KJV)
A good man leaves an inheritance to his children's children: and the wealth of the sinner is laid up for the just.

Genesis 12:2 (KJV)
And I will make of thee a great nation and I will bless thee and make thy name great; and thou shalt be a blessing:

I AM REPRESENTING GODS KINGDOM

Philippians 3:20 (KJV)
For our conversation is in heaven; from whence also we look for the Savior, the Lord Jesus Christ:

2 Corinthians 5:20 (KJV)

Now then we are ambassadors for Christ, as though God did beseech you by us: we pray you in Christ's stead, be ye reconciled to God

I AM A WINNER

Exodus 14:14 (KJV)

The LORD shall fight for you and ye shall hold your peace.

I AM DEMONSTRATING THE GIFTS OF THE SPIRIT

1 Corinthians 1:5-8 (KJV)

5 That in everything ye are enriched by him, in all utterance and in all knowledge; 6 Even as the testimony of Christ was confirmed in you: 7 So that ye come behind in no gift; waiting for the coming of our Lord Jesus Christ: 8 Who shall also confirm you unto the end, that ye may be blameless in the day of our Lord Jesus Christ.

1 Corinthians 12:4-11 (KJV)

4 Now there are diversities of gifts, but the same Spirit. 5 And there are differences of administrations, but the same Lord. 6 And there are diversities of operations, but it is the same God which worketh all in all. 7 But the manifestation of the Spirit is given to every man to profit withal. 8 For to one is given by the Spirit the word of wisdom; to another the word of knowledge by the same Spirit; 9 To another faith by the same Spirit; to another the gifts of healing by the same Spirit; 10 To another the working of miracles; to another prophecy; to another discerning of spirits; to another, divers kinds of tongues; to another the interpretation of tongues: 11 But all these

work that one and the selfsame Spirit, dividing to every man severally as he will.

I AM DISCERNING OF OPPORTUNITIES

John 9:4 (KJV)
I must work the works of him that sent me, while it is day: the night cometh, when no man can work

Ephesians 5:16 (TLB)
So be careful how you act; these are difficult days. Don't be fools; be wise: make the most of every opportunity you have for doing good.

I AM TAKING ADVANTAGE OF OPPORTUNITIES AND SUCCEEDING

Romans 8:28 (KJV)
And we know that all things work together for good to them that love God, to them who are the called according to his purpose.

I AM MAKING FULL PROOF OF MY MINISTRY

2 Timothy 4:5 (KJV)
But watch thou in all things, endure afflictions, do the work of an evangelist, make full proof of thy ministry.

I AM A SEED

Galatians 3:29 (KJV)
And if ye be Christ's, then are ye Abraham's seed and heirs according to the promise

I AM OPERATING IN INTEGRITY

Proverbs 2:7 (HCSB)

He stores up success[a] for the upright; He is a shield for those who live with integrity

I AM AWARE OF MY VALUE

Luke 12:24 (KJV)

Consider the ravens: for they neither sow nor reap; which neither have storehouse nor barn; and God feedeth them: how much more are ye better than the fowls?

Deuteronomy 8:17-18 (KJV)

17 And thou say in thine heart, my power and the might of mine hand hath gotten me this wealth. 18 But thou shalt remember the LORD thy God: for it is he that giveth thee power to get wealth that he may establish his covenant which he swore unto thy fathers, as it is this day.

I AM A LENDER

Deuteronomy 28:12-13 (NIV)

12 The LORD will open the heavens, the storehouse of his bounty, to send rain on your land in season and to bless all the work of your hands. You will lend to many nations but will borrow from none. 13 The LORD will make you the head, not the tail. If you pay attention to the commands of the LORD your God that I give you this day and carefully follow them, you will always be at the top, never at the bottom.

I AM COMPENSATED APPROPRIATELY

1 Corinthians 9:13 (NLT)
Don't you realize that those who work in the temple get their meals from the offerings brought to the temple? And those who serve at the altar get a share of the sacrificial offerings.

I AM FULL OF JOY

Psalm 16:11 (KJV)
Thou wilt shew me the path of life: in thy presence is fullness of joy; at thy right hand there are pleasures for evermore.

I AM TAKING IT BY FORCE

Matthew 11:12 (KJV)
And from the days of John the Baptist until now the kingdom of heaven suffereth violence and the violent take it by force.

I AM RECEIVED

Matthew 10:41 (KJV)
He that receiveth a prophet in the name of a prophet shall receive a prophet's reward; and he that receiveth a righteous man in the name of a righteous man shall receive a righteous man's reward.

I AM A GOOD LEADER

Matthew 20:26 (NASB)
It is not this way among you, but whoever wishes to become great among you shall be your servant.

John 3:30 (NASB)
He must increase, but I must decrease.

I AM RECEIVING 100 FOLD RETURN

Matthew 19:29 (KJV)
And every one that hath forsaken houses or brethren, or sisters or father or mother or wife or children or lands, for my name's sake, shall receive a hundredfold and shall inherit everlasting life.

I AM BLESSED TO BE A BLESSING

Galatians 6:6 (MSG)
Be very sure now, you who have been trained to a self-sufficient maturity, that you enter into a generous common life with those who have trained you, sharing all the good things that you have and experience.

I AM FEARLESS

Isaiah 54:14 (KJV)
In righteousness shalt thou be established: thou shalt be far from oppression; for thou shalt not fear: and from terror; for it shall not come near thee.

I AM LIVING APPROPRIATELY

1 Corinthians 6:19-20 (KJV)
19 What? know ye not that your body is the temple of the Holy Ghost which is in you, which ye have of God and ye are not your own? 20 For ye are bought with a price: therefore glorify God in your body and in your spirit, which are God's

I AM SURROUNDED BY ANGELS

Psalm 34:7 (KJV)
The angel of the LORD encamps round about them that fear him, and delivers them

I AM GLORIOUS TO BEHOLD

Isaiah 60:1 (KJV)
Arise, shine; for thy light is come and the glory of the LORD is risen upon thee.

I AM SOUGHT AFTER TO BLESS

Luke 6:38 (KJV)
Give and it shall be given unto you; good measure, pressed down and shaken together and running over, shall men give into your bosom. For with the same measure that ye mete withal it shall be measured to you again.

I AM IN MY SPHERE OF INFLUENCE

Matthew 5:14-16 (KJV)
14 Ye are the light of the world. A city that is set on a hill cannot be hid. 15 Neither do men light a candle and put it under a bushel, but on a candlestick; and it giveth light unto all that are in the house. 16 Let your light so shine before men, that they may see your good works and glorify your Father which is in heaven.

Ephesians 2:6-7 (KJV)
6 And hath raised us up together and made us sit together in heavenly places in Christ Jesus: 7 That in the ages to come he might shew the exceeding riches of his grace in his kindness toward us through Christ Jesus.

I AM SENSITIVE TO THE TIMES AND SEASONS

Ecclesiastes 3:1 (KJV)
To everything there is a season and a time to every purpose under the heaven.

James 4:13-15 (KJV)
13 Go to now, ye that say, today or tomorrow we will go into such a city and continue there a year and buy and sell and get gain: 14 Whereas ye know not what shall be on the morrow. For what is your life? It is even a vapor that appeared for a little time and then vanishes away. 15 For that ye ought to say, If the Lord will, we shall live and do this or that.

I AM ARISING AND ORIGINATING

Judges 7:9 (KJV)
And it came to pass the same night that the LORD said unto him, Arise, get thee down unto the host; for I have delivered it into thine hand.

Micah 4:8 (KJV)
And thou, O tower of the flock, the strong hold of the daughter of Zion, unto thee shall it come, even the first dominion; the kingdom shall come to the daughter of Jerusalem.

Ephesians 5:14 (KJV)
Wherefore he saith, awake thou that sleep and arise from the dead and Christ shall give thee light.

I AM HID UPON A ROCK

Psalm 27:5 (KJV)

For in the time of trouble he shall hide me in his pavilion: in the secret of his tabernacle shall he hide me; he shall set me up upon a rock

I AM JUSTIFIED BY FAITH

Romans 5:1-2 (KJV)

1 Therefore being justified by faith, we have peace with God through our Lord Jesus Christ: 2 By whom also we have access by faith into this grace wherein we stand, and rejoice in hope of the glory of God.

I AM MADE IN GODS IMAGE

Genesis 1:26-27 (KJV)

26 And God said, Let us make man in our image, after our likeness: and let them have dominion over the fish of the sea and over the fowl of the air and over the cattle and over all the earth and over every creeping thing that creepeth upon the earth. 27 So God created man in his own image, in the image of God created he him; male and female created he them.

I AM THAT I AM

Exodus 3:14 (KJV)

And God said unto Moses, I AM THAT I AM: and he said, Thus shalt thou say unto the children of Israel, I AM hath sent me unto you.

I Am Devotional

NOW START DECLARING

I AM WHO GOD SAYS I AM
Page 33

I AM FREE TO BE ME
Page 33

I AM FORGIVEN
Page 34

I AM FORGIVING
Page 34

I AM LIVING BY FAITH
Page 34

I AM RIGHTEOUS
Page 35

I AM A CHILD OF THE HIGHEST GOD
Page 35

I AM CONFIDENT
Page 46

I AM RECEIVING THINGS
Page 46

I AM PHYSICALLY FIT
Page 46

I AM A CHEERFUL GIVER
Page 47

I AM SUBDUING THE EARTH
Page 47

I AM ANOINTED
Page 47

I AM A LIBERAL SOUL
Page 48

I AM A REVELATOR
Page 48

I AM ACCOMPLISHED
Page 50

I AM VICTORIOUS
Page 50

I AM A GOOD STEWARD
Page 50

I AM TEACHABLE
Page 50

I AM TAUGHT OF THE HOLY SPIRIT
Page 51

I AM WEALTHY
Page 51

I AM BLAMELESS
Page 51

I AM POWERFUL
Page 51

I AM SUCCESSFUL
Page 57

I AM LIVING LIFE MORE ABUNDANTLY
Page 57

I AM LIVING IN THE OVERFLOW
Page 57

I AM RESOURCEFUL
Page 58

I AM IN RIGHT RELATIONSHIPS
Page 58

I AM LIVING A BALANCED LIFE
Page 58

I AM FREE OF BONDAGES
Page 58

I AM ADVANCING IN THE WISDOM OF GOD
Page 59

I AM HID UPON A ROCK
Page 72

I AM JUSTIFIED BY FAITH
Page 72

I AM MADE IN GODS IMAGE
Page 72

I AM THAT I AM
72

NOTES ON CHAPTER 1:
WHAT'S ON YOUR MIND

Notes on Chapter 2:

Thinking with Your Heart

Notes on Chapter 3:

Something to Prove

NOTES ON CHAPTER 4:

BE

Notes on Chapter 5:
Meditation

Notes on Chapter 6:
Heal Your Relationships

NOTES ON CHAPTER 7:

TRANSFORM YOUR MIND, TRANSFORM YOUR LIFE

YOUR
Declarations, Meditations and Scriptures

Here are the Biblical Versions used throughout

KJV – King James Version

NASB – New American Standard Bible

HCSB – Holman Christian Standard Bible

TLB – The Living Bible

ESV – English Standard Version

GW – God's Word Translation

NIV – New International Version

MSG – The Message Bible

GNT – Good News Translation